60p
net

OVEN TEMPERATURES

ELECTRIC		*GAS*
° *Celsius*	*(° Fahrenheit)*	
110°C	(225°F)	mark ¼
130°C	(250°F)	mark ½
140°C	(275°F)	mark 1
150°C	(300°F)	mark 2
160°C	(325°F)	mark 3
180°C	(350°F)	mark 4
190°C	(375°F)	mark 5
200°C	(400°F)	mark 6
220°C	(425°F)	mark 7
230°C	(450°F)	mark 8

WEIGHTS AND MEASURES

(oz = ounce, g = gramme, kg = kilogramme)

Nearest convenient Metric weight	*Imperial weight*
25g	(1oz)
50g	(2oz)
75g	(3oz)
100g	(4oz)
150g	(6oz)
200g	(8oz)
300g	(12oz)
400g	(16oz)

CAPACITY

(ml = millilitre, l = litre; ½ litre = 0·88 pint, 1 litre = 1·76 pints)

Nearest convenient Metric measure	*Imperial measure*
125ml	(¼ pt)
250ml	(½ pt)
375ml	(¾ pt)
500ml	(1 pt)

GOOD HOUSEKEEPING's

My First School Cookbook

Compiled by Good Housekeeping Institute
in conjunction with the Birds Eye Educational Service

EBURY PRESS · London

Contents

First published 1972 by
Ebury Press
Chestergate House, Vauxhall Bridge Road,
London SW1V 1HF

Photoset and printed in Great Britain by
BAS Printers Limited, Wallop, Hampshire
and bound by
James Burn (Bookbinders) Ltd,
Esher, Surrey

Introduction

In this little book you will find the recipes which form the basis of good home cooking. Almost every recipe has several variations, and these may prompt you to go on and create other dishes of your own.

The recipes are given in step-by step form, with lots of clear photographs to show the tricky points and the final result.

There's room, too, to make a few notes—for instance, you can record alterations in quantities, methods and cooking techniques as you experiment.

The recipes make enough for four people, except where different servings are indicated.

The ingredients are worked out in metric units. But, in case you need them, the equivalents in ounces and pints are also given.

Anne Dare

Head of the
Birds Eye Kitchens

Boiling

This means cooking in water at boiling point, 100°C (212°F).

Vegetables are cooked in very little water, to conserve vitamin C and flavour. The water is boiled gently, i.e., simmered, with a lid on the pan to retain the steam and speed up the cooking.

Rice and pasta are cooked in a large amount of rapidly-boiling water, to prevent sticking. Because these foods boil over easily, leave the lid off the pan.

VEGETABLES

(*See photos* A *and* B)

Wash vegetables well, peel, trim and cut up as required. Use as little water as possible, salt it, bring to a fast boil and add the prepared vegetables. Cook with the lid on the pan, timing carefully—over-cooked vegetables lose flavour and texture. Here are the times:

	mins.
Brussels Sprouts	15–20
Cabbage, shredded	2–3
Cauliflower, whole	20
—broken into florets	10
Carrots, whole	20
—sliced or diced	10
Celery, cut in 2-in. lengths	10–15
Onions, whole	45
Parsnips	30–45
Peas, shelled	10–20
Potatoes, cut into even-sized pieces	15–20
Runner Beans, sliced	15–20
Swedes	20–40
Turnips	20–40

Frozen vegetables: cook according to the manufacturers' instructions.

Drain all vegetables and serve immediately, with a knob of butter or margarine (*photo* C). A sprinkling of chopped parsley looks attractive.

BOILED RICE

Water
Salt
40g long-grain rice (1½oz) per person

1. Boil a large pan of salted water.
2. When it is boiling, add the rice and cook for 12–15 mins. Test by biting a grain to see if it is cooked—the rice should still be firm, but not 'powdery'.
3. Pour the contents of the pan into a sieve and shake to separate.
4. Leave to drain well.
5. To keep the rice hot (if necessary), put in a warm oven on a baking sheet, covered with foil.

PASTA (e.g., Spaghetti, Macaroni)

Water
Salt
40g spaghetti (1½ oz) per person

1. Heat a large pan of salted water.
2. When the water boils, place the ends of the spaghetti in the water and hold until they become pliable (*photo* D).
3. Coil the spaghetti round in the pan.
4. Boil for 15–20 mins. until soft.
5. Drain the spaghetti in a sieve (*photo* E).
6. Toss it in the pan with a knob of butter.

BOILED EGGS

Use eggs at room temperature, to prevent the shells cracking. Allow 1–2 eggs per person (*photo* F).

1. Lower the eggs gently into a pan a quarter full of boiling water, cover.
2. Cooking times: soft-boiled, 3–4 mins., hard-boiled, 10 mins.
3. Cool hard-boiled eggs immediately under cold running water—this prevents a black ring round the yolk.

Uses: Whole or halved, in Egg Mayonnaise; sliced (*photo* G), in salads or sandwiches, or as a garnish.

A

B

C

D

E

F

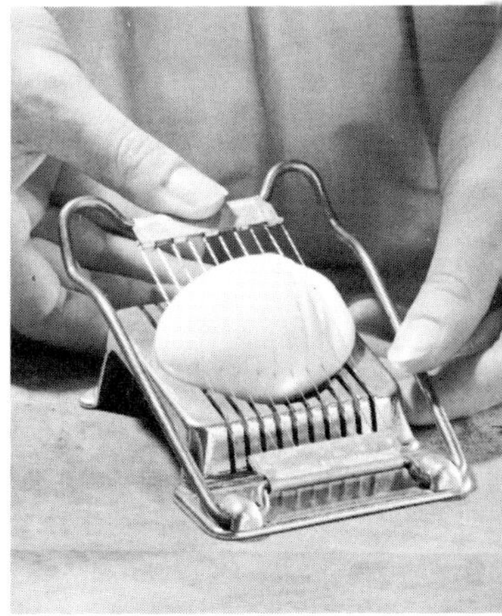

G

Shallow Fat Frying

Cooking in hot shallow fat, usually in a wide, shallow frying pan. This is a quick method, suitable only for small pieces of food which need little cooking. Sometimes no fat is required, e.g., when bacon is fried in its own fat. Normally the fat comes about one-third of the way up the side of the food. The food must be well cooked on both sides and then thoroughly drained.

Frying is sometimes used as a preliminary treatment for the meat and/or vegetables in stews or casseroles: the term for this is sautéing.

FRIED EGGS AND BACON

Allow 2 rashers of bacon and 1–2 eggs per person.

1. Cut the rind off the rashers, using kitchen scissors, and snip into the fat to prevent curling during cooking.
2. Lay the bacon flat in the frying pan (*photo* A). You can overlap very lean parts on top of the fat part of the next rasher; more of the fat is then in contact with the pan base and no extra fat is needed.
3. Cook gently at first to melt the fat, and then more quickly, on both sides, until well done.
4. The eggs may be cooked in the bacon fat or in a little melted cooking fat or oil.
5. Break each egg separately into a cup and slide it carefully into the hot fat *photo* B).
6. Tilt the pan slightly so that the egg lies in a pool of hot fat at one side. Lower the pan as soon as the white sets into shape. To cook the upper side, either baste with hot fat from the pan or turn the egg over with a fish slice (*photo* C).

FRIED FISH FILLETS

Before fish is fried it is usual to coat it, to help retain the shape, moisture and flavour during cooking. The coating can be seasoned flour, or egg and crumbs.

Plaice in Breadcrumbs

4 fillets of plaice
1 egg, beaten
Salt and pepper
White breadcrumbs
50g cooking fat or oil (2oz)
Lemon slices or wedges

1. Wipe the fillets.
2. Brush with beaten egg (*photo* D), season and coat with crumbs (*photo* E); an alternative method is to place the crumbs in a polythene bag, put in the fish and then shake gently.
3. Heat the fat and fry the fillets for 2–3 mins. on each side, until golden-brown; allow time for the fat to re-heat after adding each fillet (*photo* F).
4. Drain well on absorbent paper, and serve with lemon and a pat of parsley butter (*photo* G).

FROZEN FOODS

Fish Fingers, Fish Cakes, Fish Steaks in breadcrumbs, Beefburgers and Steaklets are all shallow-fat-fried. For correct timing, follow the manufacturers' pack instructions. All these foods can be cooked straight from frozen.

A

B

C

D

E

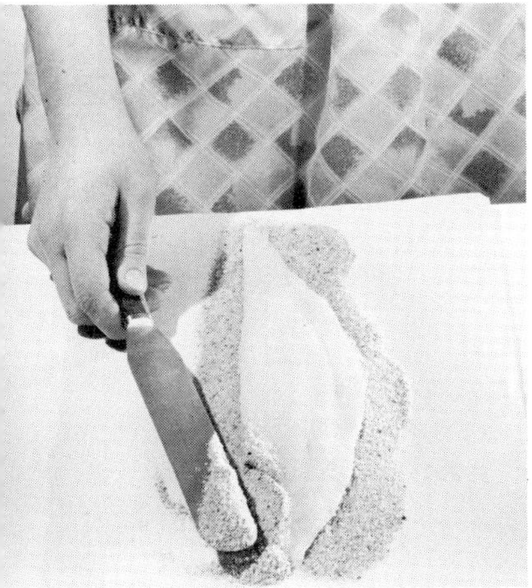

F

G

Shallow Fat Frying —Omelettes

Omelettes are easy, quick to prepare, versatile and suitable either for a quick snack or as the main course of a meal. They are a good source of protein and can be varied in many ways.

Special 7–8-in. omelette pans with curved sides are made, and should be kept only for omelettes; alternatively, use any frying pan.

BASIC OMELETTE RECIPE
(for one person)

2 eggs
Salt and pepper
15g butter or margarine (½oz)

1. Break the eggs into a basin and beat lightly with a fork (*photo* A).
2. Add 2 tbsps water and some salt and pepper, and mix well.
3. Melt the butter in a frying pan over medium heat.
4. Pour in the egg mixture (*photo* B) and stir gently with the back of a fork (or a wooden spatula if the pan is non-stick).
5. Draw in the sides of the omelette mixture to the centre (*photo* C) so that the liquid egg can flow to the sides and so cook.
6. When the eggs start to set, stop stirring and leave the pan until the omelette is set and the underside golden-brown. At this stage, place any flavourings or fillings on top (*photo* D).
7. Turn one side of the omelette one-third over towards the centre, then fold over the opposite side (*photo* E).
8. Tip it out on to a hot plate, so that the folded sides are underneath, and serve at once (*photos* F *and* G).

VARIATIONS
Unless otherwise directed, add filling before folding omelette.

(*a*) **Cheese**—add 50g grated cheese (2oz).
(*b*) **Mushroom**—add 50g sliced mushrooms (2oz), sautéed in a little butter.
(*c*) **Tomato**—sauté 2 chopped tomatoes in a little butter, season well, mix in a pinch of mixed herbs or garlic salt.
(*d*) **Smoked Haddock**—Mix a little flaked cooked haddock with a little butter.
(*e*) **Sweet Corn**—add 50g cooked sweet corn (2oz), with a little chopped red pepper if liked.
(*f*) **Spanish Omelette**—Sauté a little chopped onion, any diced cooked potato, a sliced tomato and 25g cooked peas (1oz); add the egg mixture and a pinch of mixed herbs. Cook slowly, shaking the pan occasionally, until the egg is set. Place the pan under the grill to brown the top. Serve without folding.

A

B

C

D

E

F

G

Deep Fat Frying

To cook food in hot deep fat, you need a deep-fat 'bath' or a strong saucepan which is 10–15cm deep (4–5in). A wire draining basket is useful when cooking more than one item.

Oil is best for deep frying, as it can be heated to a high temperature without flavouring the food. Half-fill the pan and heat slowly. Test the temperature by frying a cube of bread: if it turns golden-brown in 50 seconds, then the fat is ready to begin frying. Remember that the fat is at a temperature of 180–200°C (340–390°F), which is much hotter than boiling water, so always take care.

Deep fat frying is most often used for cooking chipped potatoes.

CHIPS

1. Wash and peel old potatoes, slice and then cut into chips (*photos* A *and* B). Dry well on kitchen paper.
2. Slowly heat the fat and test by dropping in a chip—if this rises to the surface straight away, surrounded by bubbles, the fat is ready to use.
3. Put the chips in a frying basket and lower carefully into the fat; cook until golden-brown and tender (*photo* C).
4. Drain the chips well on absorbent kitchen paper and serve immediately, in an uncovered dish.

Other foods which are deep fat fried usually require a coating; e.g., fish in batter, fruit fritters and potato croquettes. The coating is added to protect the food during cooking and keep it moist. (For recipe for fish in batter see p. 38.)

Many frozen foods can be deep fat fried, e.g., chips, potato croquettes, cod fillets and fish fingers in batter. Fry these while still frozen, according to the manufacturers' pack instructions.

FRUIT FRITTERS

A small can of pineapple rings
125ml coating batter (1/4 pint); see p. 38
Oil or fat for frying
Caster sugar

1. Drain the can of pineapple rings.
2. Using a skewer or fork, dip each ring in batter till well coated (*photo* D).
3. Lower the ring carefully into the preheated fat, without splashing.
4. Turn once during the cooking and fry until golden-brown; 2–3 may be cooked at once, depending on the size of the pan (*photo* E).
5. Using a draining spoon, remove from pan; drain well on absorbent paper.
6. Dredge with caster sugar and serve at once (*photo* F). A sauce can be made with the pineapple juice thickened with arrowroot—see p. 32.

Variations: Use peaches, apricots, apple rings or halves of banana in same way.

RULES FOR DEEP FAT FRYING

1. Use a heavy pan, only half-full.
2. Use clean fat or oil; don't overheat.
3. All foods must be coated in batter or crumbs unless it is starchy, e.g., chips.
4. Make sure food is dry before adding.
5. Take safety precautions:
   Don't let fat drip down outside of pan, or it will catch fire.
   Turn the pan handle inwards.
   Have a baking sheet or lid nearby in case of fire.
   Don't let any water from pan lids drop into the hot fat.
   Cool fat before straining.

A

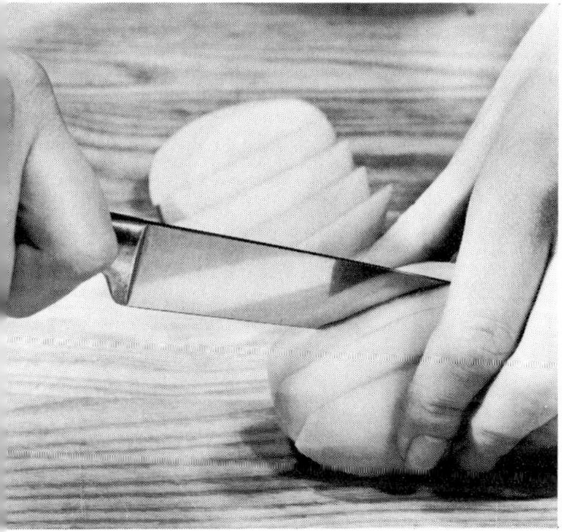

B

C

D

E

F

Roasting

Correctly speaking, roasting is cooking on a spit in front of, or over, a glowing heat. Nowadays, it is the term used for the cooking of meat or poultry in hot fat in the oven; potatoes and parsnips may also be cooked in this way.

Method for Roasting Meat or Poultry

1. Trim and wipe the joint or prepare the bird. Stuff it if necessary.
2. Weigh the prepared joint or bird and calculate the cooking time.
3. Put the meat or poultry in a shallow oven tin, and put some extra fat on top if the meat is particularly lean.
4. Roast in the centre of the oven for the correct time, basting frequently.
5. Meat is moister if cooked in a covered roasting tin or under kitchen foil—this helps stop shrinkage and also keeps the oven clean. However, the flavour and colour will not be as good.
6. Meat can be roasted by a quick or slow method—see chart.

SUITABLE JOINTS AND POULTRY

Beef: Sirloin, rib, topside, brisket.
Accompaniments: Yorkshire pudding, gravy, horseradish sauce or mustard, roast potatoes.

Lamb: Loin, leg, shoulder, breast—stuffed and rolled.
Accompaniments: Mint sauce or jelly, stuffing, redcurrent jelly, onion sauce, gravy, roast potatoes.

Pork: Loin, blade, spare rib, fillet.
Accompaniments: Apple sauce, sage & onion stuffing, gravy, roast potatoes.

Chicken: Either fresh or frozen.
Accompaniments: Sausage-meat stuffing, bacon rolls, bread sauce, gravy, roast potatoes.

GRAVY

Thin gravy is easily made by just adding 250ml (½pt) water from boiled vegetables to the sediments left from the joint, and seasoning to taste. Thicker gravy can be made with Bisto or Gravy Mix by following the manufacturers' pack instructions.

MEAT, POULTRY	QUICK METHOD	SLOW METHOD
	Oven temperature 220°C (425°F) mark 7	Oven temperature 180°C (350°F) mark 4
Beef and Lamb	15 mins. per 400g (1lb), plus 15 mins. for small joints 20 mins. per 400g (1lb), plus 20 mins. for joints with bones 25 mins. per 400g (1lb), plus 25 mins. if boned and rolled	20 mins. per 400g (1lb), plus 20 mins. 27 mins. per 400g (1lb), plus 27 mins. 33 mins. per 400 g (1lb), plus 33 mins.
Pork	25 mins. per 400g (1lb), plus 25 mins. for joints with bones 30 mins. per 400g (1lb), plus 30 mins. for rolled boned joints	All joints are roasted for 40 mins. per 400g (1lb), plus 40 mins.
Chicken	Frozen chicken—cook according to manufacturer's pack instructions, but *do thaw out properly first.*	20 mins. per 400g (1lb), plus 20 mins.

Carving Roast Meat and Chicken

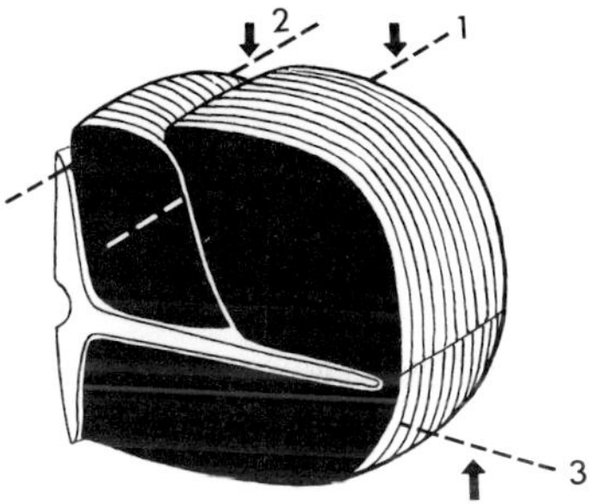

Sirloin of Beef: Remove flank by cutting down at 1, and along bone; slice as shown. Remove and carve fillet (2) in same way. Turn joint and carve uppercut (3).

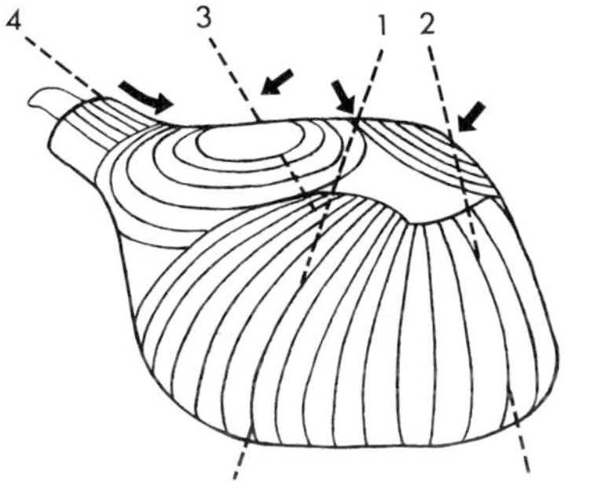

Shoulder of Lamb or Pork: Take first cut at 1, slicing in direction shown by arrow; follow with 2, 3 and 4.

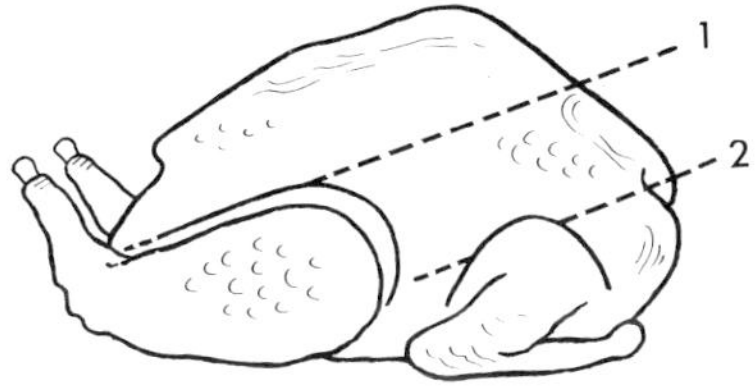

Chicken I: Remove first the leg then the wing on one side; carve slices from these joints, if large enough.

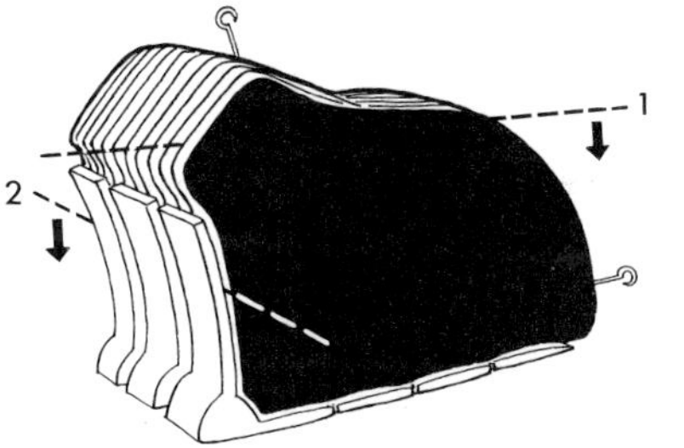

Back Rib of Beef: Slice down at 1 in direction of arrow. If necessary, detach meat from bones at 2.

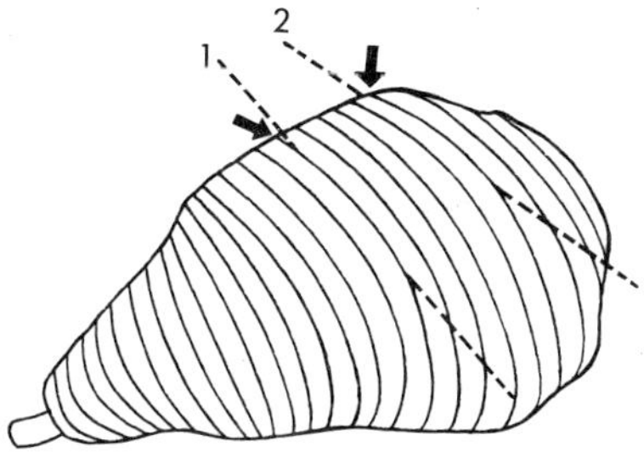

Leg of Lamb or Pork: Take first cut at 1, and second cut at 2, then slice between these points; finally work outwards.

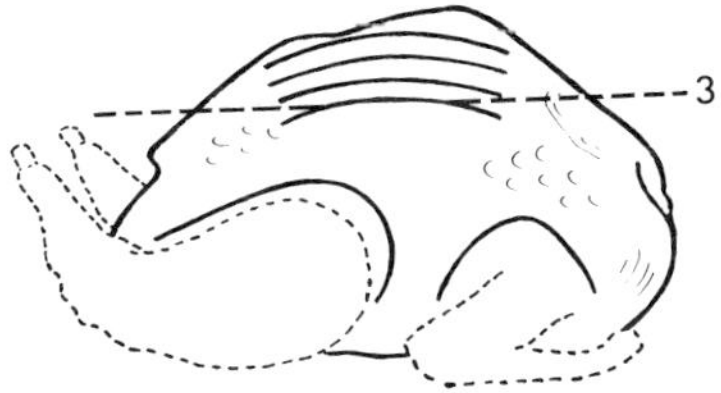

Chicken II: Slice breast meat, then rest of bird. Serve each person with some white and some dark meat, plus stuffing.

Stewing

Long, slow cooking, in a measured amount of simmering liquid; the liquor is always served with the cooked food. This method is useful for producing dishes from the tougher, cheaper cuts of meat, which are made tender during cooking. Stewing for long periods is easier in a casserole in the oven, especially when an auto-timer can be used.

There are two basic types of stew—brown and white. A brown stew is coloured by sautéing the meat, vegetables and flour before adding the liquid—this gives a fuller, richer flavour.

WHITE STEW: IRISH STEW

400g middle neck of mutton or lamb (1lb)
600g potatoes, peeled (1½lb)
2 onions and carrots, peeled
Salt and pepper
250ml water (½pt)
Chopped parsley

Oven temperature 180°C (350°F), mark 4

1. Cut the meat into chops if necessary (*photo* A), and cut off excess fat.
2. Slice the potatoes and onions (and carrots, if included—*photo* B).
3. Place alternate layers of meat, potato and onion in a casserole or saucepan, finishing with a layer of potato, and seasoning each layer (*photos* C *and* D).
4. Add the water; put on the lid and cook in the centre of the oven (or on top of the stove) for 2–2½ hrs.
5. Garnish with parsley before serving (*photo* G).

Variation: Lancashire Hot-pot: use 8 best end of neck cutlets and add 2 lamb's kidneys, cored and sliced.

BROWN STEW: BEEF GOULASH

600g chuck steak (1½lb)
Seasoned flour
2 tbsps. oil
1 onion, peeled and thinly sliced
250ml stock (¼pt)
A 395-g can of tomatoes (14oz)
1 tsp tomato purée
100g frozen peas (4oz)
2 level tsps paprika pepper
2 tbsps natural yoghurt (optional)

Oven temperature 180°C (350°F), mark 4

1. Cut the meat into 3-cm cubes (1-in) and coat with seasoned flour (*photo* E).
2. Heat the oil in a saucepan or casserole and quickly brown the meat on all sides, then remove from the pan (*photo* F).
3. Sauté the onion in the oil until clear.
4. Put the meat, stock, tomatoes and tomato purée in a casserole and cook in the centre of the oven for about 1¾ hrs, or simmer in a saucepan on top of the stove.
5. Add the peas and paprika and cook for a further 10 mins.
6. Remove from the heat, stir in the yoghurt, if used, and serve at once.

A

B

C

D

E

F

G

Casseroles Made With Chicken

Chicken, both whole and in joints, is available all the year round and is relatively cheap. Frozen chicken must be completely thawed before use. Chicken casserole in many forms can provide economical meals for the whole family.

CASSEROLE OF CHICKEN AND TOMATOES

2 onions, peeled and sliced
100g mushrooms, sliced (4oz)
50g bacon, chopped (2oz)
1 tbsp oil
25g butter (1oz)
4 chicken joints
3 level tbsps flour
370ml chicken stock (¾ pt)
A 425-g can of tomatoes (15-oz)
Salt and pepper

Oven temperature 180°C (350°F), mark 4

1. Lightly fry prepared onions, mushrooms and bacon in oil in a frying pan for about 5 mins., until golden-brown (*photos* A *and* B).
2. Remove from the pan and place in a casserole.
3. Fry the chicken joints for 5 mins., until golden-brown.
4. Put the chicken on top of the vegetables in the casserole (*photo* C).
5. Stir the flour into the remaining fat and cook for 2–3 mins.; gradually stir in the stock and bring to the boil; stir until thick.
6. Add the tomatoes and season to taste (*photo* D).
7. Pour the sauce into the casserole, cover and cook in the centre of the oven for ¾–1 hour, until the chicken is tender (*photo* E).

Note: If you wish, all the frying can be done in the casserole, provided this is flameproof.

CHICKEN CURRY

2 onions, peeled and sliced
50g butter (2oz)
4 chicken joints
1 apple, peeled, cored and chopped
2 level tsps curry powder
2 level tbsps seasoned flour
125ml stock (¼ pt)
A little lemon juice
2 level tsps sweet chutney

Oven temperature 180°C (350°F), mark 4

1. Fry the onions in the butter in a large flameproof casserole, remove.
2. Add the chicken joints and fry until golden.
3. Add the apple, curry powder and flour, stir well and cook for 1–2 mins.
4. Add the stock, lemon juice, onions and chutney and mix together.
5. Cover the casserole, place in the centre of the oven and cook for ¾–1 hour, until the chicken is tender.
6. Serve with 150g rice (6oz), boiled as directed on p. 4.

A

B

C

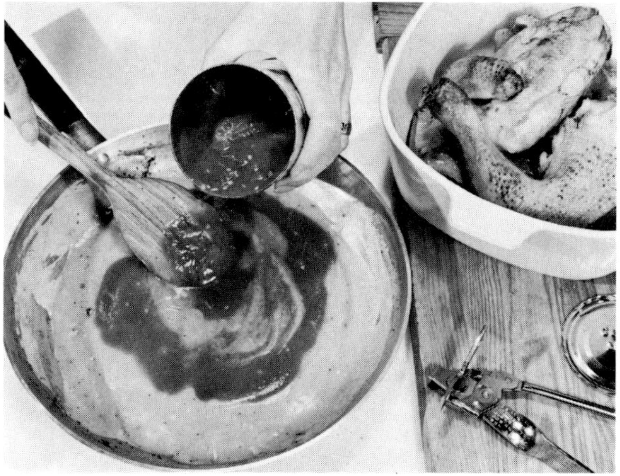

D

E

Grilling

Grilling is a quick method of cooking by radiant heat. Suitable foods include tender cuts of meat and other small items, e.g., steak, chops, liver, kidney, gammon, bacon, sausages, fish (whole, filleted or in steaks), mushrooms and tomatoes. Anything to be grilled is usually not more than 1 in. thick.

To Grill Meat

1. Trim off any excess fat (*photo* A).
2. Pre-heat the grill for about 5 mins.
3. Place the meat on the grill rack.
4. Brush with oil or melted butter and season well. Grill, turning frequently, until cooked. Steak can be served rare, medium or well-done by varying the time from 5 to 15 mins. Pork and lamb chops are better thoroughly cooked, for 15–20 mins.

Accompaniments for Grilled Meat

Grilled halved tomatoes
Grilled or sautéed mushrooms
Pototo chips or matchsticks
Jacket potatoes
Green or tomato salad
Peas and sweet corn
Grilled apple or pineapple rings (with pork chops or gammon rashers)

MIXED GRILL

4 best end of neck lamb cutlets
200g sausages (½lb)
2 lambs' kidneys
4 rashers of bacon (rind removed)
4 tomatoes, halved
4 mushrooms, washed and trimmed
Melted butter or oil
Salt and pepper

1. Pre-heat the grill.
2. Prepare the chops by wiping and trimming.
3. Separate the sausages and prick with a fork.
4. Halve the kidneys and remove the core (*photo* B).
5. Place all the meat and the bacon on the grill rack, and the tomatoes and mushrooms below in the grill pan.
6. Brush the ingredients with butter or oil and season well (*photo* C).
7. Grill, turning the food frequently to ensure even cooking (*photo* D). Allow 14–16 mins. cooking time overall, removing cooked items to a warm platter when ready.
8. Serve all the food together on a large platter, garnished with watercress (*photo* E).

KEBABS

Make kebabs by threading an assortment of small pieces of food on to skewers and grill. Any of the following foods may be used: lean pieces of lamb, steak, ham, bacon, kidney, liver, sausages, apple, banana, pineapple, tomato, red and green peppers, onion.

Suggested combinations:

Lamb, onion and bay leaves
Ham and pineapple
Bacon rolls, banana and tomato
Luncheon meat, mushrooms and pineapple.

1. Pre-heat the grill. (An automatic spit roaster with a kebab attachment gives excellent results, as it rotates at an even rate.)
2. Thread the items alternately the length of 4 skewers.
3. Brush with oil or melted butter and season well.
4. Place the skewers on the grill rack under the grill.
5. Grill under a moderate heat, turning frequently, for about 5 mins., or until all the food is cooked.
6. Serve with boiled rice and a green salad (*photo* F).

A

B

C

D

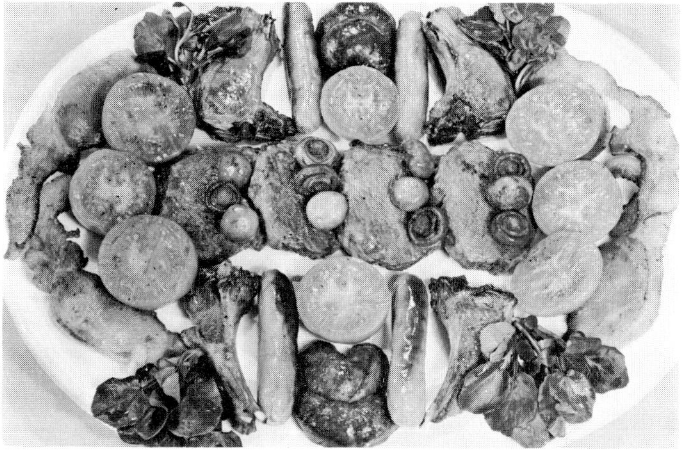

E

F

Shepherd's Pie and Fish Pie

These are useful dishes for main meals or snacks, and can be easily varied.

SHEPHERD'S PIE

600g potatoes (1½lb)
2-3 tbsps milk
25g margarine (1oz)
Salt and pepper
1 large onion, peeled
25g cooking fat (1oz)
300g minced meat (12oz)
1 level tbsp flour
1 stock cube
250ml water (½pt)

Oven temperature 200°C (425°F), mark 7

1. Grease an ovenproof pie dish (2-pt).
2. Peel and boil the potatoes, then mash with the milk, margarine, salt and pepper (*photo* A).
3. Chop the onion and fry in the fat until soft—stir to prevent sticking (*photo* B).
4. Add the meat and continue to fry until brown (*photo* C).
5. Sprinkle in the flour and stir well (*photo* D).
6. Add the stock cube and water gradually and mix well.
7. Simmer for 10 mins., then season.
8. Put into the prepared dish and pile the potato evenly on top (*photos* E *and* F). Smooth with a palette knife and mark the surface with a fork.
9. Bake at the top of the oven until the potato is golden-brown—approx. 25–30 mins. Serve hot, garnished with tomato or parsley (*photo* G).

VARIATIONS

(*a*) Replace the meat with corned beef.
(*b*) Add 3 level tsps curry powder and 25g sultanas (1oz).
(*c*) Make a Greek version by layering slices of potato and tomato with the meat and covering the whole with a cheese sauce (see p. 30); top with 50g grated cheese (2oz).

FISH PIE

600g potatoes (1½lb)
2-3 tbsps milk
25g butter or margarine (1oz)
Salt and pepper
300g poached cod (12oz)
375ml cheese sauce (¾pt)
100g frozen peas (4oz)
1 tomato, sliced

Oven temperature 200°C (425°F), mark 7

1. Grease an ovenproof pie dish (2-pt).
2. Peel and boil the potatoes and mash with the milk and butter; season well.
3. Flake the cod into an ovenproof dish and pour the sauce over.
4. Add the frozen peas and cover with the potato. Smooth with a palette knife and mark the top with a fork.
5. Bake at the top of the oven until the potato is golden-brown—approx. 25–30 mins.
6. Serve hot, garnished with the tomato.

A

B

C

D

E

F

G

Salads and Dressings

Salads can be as varied as the number of vegetables available. During summer the ingredients to use are lettuce, tomatoes, radish, cucumber, watercress, etc. Although these are available more or less throughout the year, they are usually more expensive in winter, so it is cheaper to use, say, cabbage, celery and onions, and make a Cole Slaw.

Serve salads to accompany cold meats and fish. A green salad is often served with steak or other hot dishes when something with a crisp texture is preferred to cooked vegetables.

All salads are improved by the addition of a dressing, to aid digestion and add flavour.

MIXED SUMMER SALAD

1 lettuce
1 bunch of watercress
4 tomatoes
½ **a cucumber**
A bunch of spring onions

1. Wash all the vegetables well in cold water (*photos* A *and* B).
2. Drain well in a colander or by shaking in a tea towel or basket (*photo* C).
3. Trim all the salad ingredients carefully:
   Lettuce: separate the leaves and divide into equal-sized pieces, removing any brown parts.
   Watercress: trim stalks to about 2 in. and remove any discoloured leaves.
   Tomatoes: slice, or cut into segments.
   Cucumber: slice or chop into ½-in. dice (peel if you wish).
   Spring onions: cut off the root and trim the green tops to about 2 in.; leave whole, or snip with scissors into rings, and serve sprinkled over salads.
4. Serve all the vegetables either tossed together in a wooden bowl, or arranged attractively on a platter.

COLE SLAW

¼ **of a hard white cabbage**
½ **a green pepper (optional)**
3 sticks of celery
1 red-skinned eating apple
1 small onion
2 tbsps salad cream or mayonnaise

1. Shred cabbage finely, across leaves.
2. Cut the pepper into thin strips.
3. Chop the celery.
4. Core and slice the apple (do not peel).
5. Peel and slice the onion thinly.
6. Mix all the ingredients together and bind with the salad cream or mayonnaise (*see large photo*).

FRENCH SALAD DRESSING

½ **level tsp salt**
¼ **level tsp pepper**
½ **level tsp dry mustard**
½ **level tsp sugar**
1 tbsp vinegar
2 tbsps olive or salad oil

1. Put the salt, pepper, mustard and sugar in a basin (*photo* D).
2. Blend in oil, using a fork (*photo* E).
3. Add vinegar and mix well (*photo* F).
   Alternatively, place all the ingredients in a screw-topped jar and shake well.

This basic recipe can be varied by adding freshly chopped herbs, gherkins, pickles or ½ tsp French mustard.

SALAD CREAM

Some people prefer a cream instead of a dressing with their salad. Bought salad cream can be 'dressed up' by adding chopped herbs, lemon juice, capers, tomato purée, grated onion or cheese.

A

B

C

D

E

F

G

Suet Pastry

Suet is such a hard fat that it can only be added to a mixture in the form of small granules. The method of making suet pastry does not incorporate air, so self-raising flour must be used.

Suet Pastry (Basic Recipe)
200g self-raising flour (8oz)
1 level tsp salt (use only ½ tsp for sweet dishes)
100g suet (4oz)
125ml water (¼ pt)

1. Sift the flour and salt into a bowl, stir in the suet and add nearly all the water, to make a soft, elastic dough. If necessary, add the remaining water.
2. Knead lightly and roll out to the required shape.

STEAK AND KIDNEY PUDDING

Suet pastry as above
450g stewing steak (1lb), cut into small pieces)
1 sheep's kidney, skinned, cored and cut into small pieces
2 level tbsps flour mixed with salt and pepper (seasoned flour)
1 onion, peeled and chopped
4 tbsps stock or water

1. Boil some water in a steamer or saucepan (1 tsp vinegar will prevent aluminium pans from staining).
2. Grease a 750-ml pudding basin (1½-pt).
3. Roll out the pastry into a round 5cm (2 in.) larger than the diameter of the basin, cut out a quarter of it and keep for the lid (*photo* A).
4. Line the pudding basin with the rest of the pastry; damp and overlap the cut edges.
5. Toss the meat and kidney in the seasoned flour. Mix with the onion and put into the basin (*photo* B).
6. Add 4 tbsps stock or water.
7. Roll out the lid, damp the top edges of the pastry and press on, sealing carefully (*photo* C).
8. Cover with greaseproof paper or foil (*photo* D) and steam for 3½–4 hours.
9. Serve in the basin, which is traditionally wrapped in a napkin (*photo* E).

Don't let the steamer boil dry.

JAM ROLY-POLY

Roll out the suet pastry dough to an oblong. Spread with jam to within 3cm (1 in) of the edges. Moisten the edges and roll up. Wrap in greaseproof paper or foil and steam for 2–2½ hours, or boil for 1½ hours. Serve with custard sauce.

FRUIT LAYER PUDDING

Suet pastry as above
400g fruit (1lb)
100g sugar (4oz)

Shape the dough into a roll and cut into 4 graduated slices. Roll out each separately in sizes to fit a 1½-pt pudding basin. Place the smallest piece in the basin and put a layer of prepared fruit and sugar over it. Repeat in this way until you finish with a layer of pastry. Cover, and steam for 2 hours.

Use rhubarb, plums, damsons, cherries, apricots, or sliced apple and a little orange rind; golden syrup with breadcrumbs, jam and mincemeat also make good fillings.

Canned pie fillings are quick and easy to use and make a very good pudding.

A

B

C

D

E

Shortcrust Pastry

This pastry, as its name suggests, should be crisp and 'short', i.e., crumbly. It is widely used for both savoury and sweet dishes. The fat is incorporated with the flour by rubbing-in.

Basic Recipe

100g plain flour (4oz)
½ level tsp salt (less for sweet dishes)
25g lard (1oz)
25g margarine (1oz)
4–6 tsps cold water to mix

1. Sift the flour and salt into a mixing bowl.
2. Add the fat to the flour, cutting up into small pieces. Rub into the flour with cool fingertips until the mixture resembles breadcrumbs and there are no large lumps (*photo* A). Avoid over-rubbing, which is detected by the mixture turning yellow.
3. Add the water a tsp. at a time, and mix with a round-bladed knife until the mixture sticks together (*photo* B).
4. Using one hand, knead it lightly into a smooth, firm dough (*photo* C).
5. Roll out on a lightly floured surface, and use as required.

INDIVIDUAL JAM TARTLETS

Short crust pastry as above
Jam

MAKES 10–12
Oven temperature 220°C (425°F) mark 7

1. Roll out the pastry thinly.
2. Cut into rounds, using a 7-cm fluted cutter (2 ½-inch) (*photo* D).
3. Ease the rounds into tartlet tins, press down firmly (*photo* E) and prick the base.
4. Fill each pastry case one-third full with jam (*photo* F) and bake towards the top of the oven for 10–15 mins.
5. Remove from tins and cool on a wire rack.

Variations: Use marmalade, mincemeat or lemon curd for the filling.

Meringue Tarts

Fill with lemon curd and bake at 190°C (375°F) mark 5 for 15 mins. Reduce to 150°C (300°F) mark 2, cover with meringue (see page 58) and bake for a further 10 mins.

Custard Tarts

Shortcrust pastry as above
250ml milk (½pt)
13g sugar (½oz)
2 eggs
Nutmeg

Oven temperature 190°C (375°F) mark 5

1. Make pastry cases, using 12 patty tins.
2. Heat the milk to blood heat.
3. Put the sugar and the eggs into a basin and beat well together.
4. Pour the milk onto the eggs, and stir.
5. Strain the mixture into a jug and two-thirds fill the lined patty tins. Sprinkle with grated nutmeg.
6. Bake in the centre of the oven for 15 mins.
7. Reduce the heat to 180°C (350°F) mark 4, and continue cooking until the custard is set.

Savoury Tarts

Make as above, but add 50g (2oz) onion, finely chopped and sautéed, and 50g (2oz) bacon, finely diced and sautéed; omit the sugar, and season to taste.

A

B

C

D

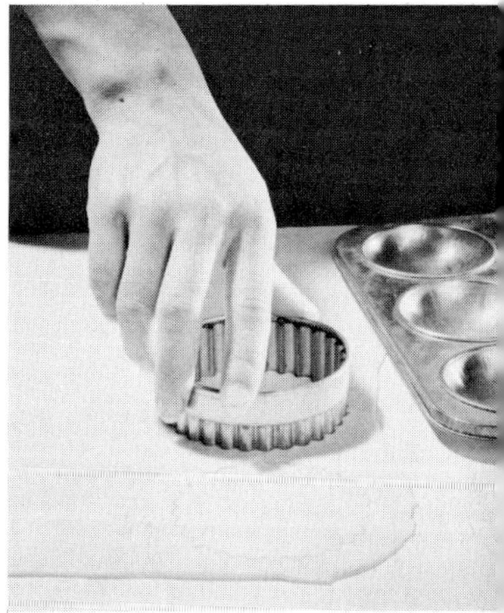

E

F

Jam Tarts

Shortcrust Pastry-Pies

You can use bought shortcrust pastry for speed, or make your own.

SINGLE-CRUST FRUIT PIE

Shortcrust pastry, as in basic recipe, or a 7½-oz pkt of frozen pastry, thawed
600g cooking apples (1½lb)
100g sugar (4oz)
1 level tsp ground cinnamon (optional)
Caster sugar

Oven temperature 220°C (425°F), mark 7

1. Use a 1½-pt oval pie dish. Roll out the pastry into an oval 3cm (1in.) larger than the top of the dish.
2. Turn the dish upside-down on the pastry and cut through the pastry about 1cm (½in.) away from the edge of the dish (*photo* A).
3. Damp the edges of the dish and cover with strips cut from the trimmings of the pastry.
4. Peel, core and slice the apples.
5. Layer the apples, sugar and cinnamon in the dish.
6. Damp the pastry edges, lift the lid on the rolling pin and place it in position without stretching; seal the edges well.
7. Make horizontal cuts into the edge of the pie all the way round, holding down the pastry with the back of your first finger (*photo* B). Mark vertical decorations with the prongs of a fork.
8. Brush the pastry with water and sprinkle with caster sugar.
9. Bake near the top of the oven for 10 mins. Reduce the temperature to 180°C (350°F), mark 4, and cook for a further 20–30 mins., till fruit is tender. Serve hot or cold, with custard or cream.

DOUBLE-CRUST BACON-EGG PIE

150g streaky bacon (6oz), rinded
2 eggs
2 tbsps milk
Salt and pepper
Extra milk to glaze the pastry
150g plain flour (6oz)
½ level tsp salt
75g lard (3oz) or half each lard and margarine
Cold water to mix

Oven temperature 200°C (400°F), mark 6

1. Prepare the pastry (see basic recipe).
2. Chop the bacon into small pieces.
3. Break eggs into a basin, whisk lightly, then stir in milk and seasoning.
4. Divide the pastry evenly into 2 pieces and roll out one on a floured surface into a round a little bigger than a 21-cm (7-in.) pie plate. Line the plate.
5. Put the bacon on the pastry and pour the egg mixture over (*photo* C).
6. Roll out the remaining pastry to fit the top of the plate and put in position, damping the edges before pressing together (*photo* D); trim edges.
7. Hold down edges of pastry with back of forefinger and make horizontal cuts along edge, then pull in edges of pastry every 3cm (1in.) to scallop.
8. Brush with milk (*photo* E).
9. Put pie on baking tray and bake near top of oven for about 30 mins.

VARIATIONS

(*a*) Cheese and Onion Pie: Fill with 2 large onions, chopped and cooked, mixed with 200g grated cheese (8oz), 1 egg, beaten, and salt and pepper.
(*b*) Use steak and kidney pie filling.

A

B

C

D

E

F

Roux Sauces

These can be adapted for coating food, or to pour from a jug. This is done simply by varying the amount of fat and flour added to each 500ml milk (1pt).

Pouring Sauce

40g butter or margarine (1½oz)
40g flour (1½oz)
500ml milk (1pt)
Salt, pepper, mustard

Coating Sauce

50g butter or margarine (2oz)
50g flour (2oz)
500ml milk (1pt)
Salt, pepper, mustard

1. Melt the fat in a saucepan. Add the flour and mix well with a wooden spoon (*photo* A).
2. Cook until the mixture bubbles, then remove from the heat (*photo* B).
3. Add the milk a little at a time, stirring thoroughly before adding any more (*photo* C).
4. Return the pan to the heat and bring to the boil, stirring all the time, until the sauce thickens. Beat well to make the sauce glossy (*photo* D). Season to taste.

Cheese Sauce

Add 75g grated cheese (3oz), a pinch of dry mustard and a few drops of Worcestershire sauce, and beat well into the sauce, until smooth. Don't re-heat, or the cheese will become stringy.

Use for macaroni or cauliflower cheese, or as a sauce for cooked chicken joints or grilled fish, etc. (*photo* E).

Parsley Sauce

Add 2 tbsps chopped parsley and a little lemon juice, stir thoroughly and re-heat.

Use to accompany fish or gammon; it can also be used with carrots.

Mushroom Sauce

Add 50g (2oz) sliced sautéed button mushrooms to the finished sauce and cook for 2-3 mins.

Serve with cooked chicken or fish.

TUNA AND MACARONI CRISP

100g macaroni (4oz) cooked (see p. 4)
A 198-g can of tuna (7-oz)
250ml white sauce (½pt)
75g grated cheese (3oz)
Salt and pepper
A small pkt of potato crisps

Oven temperature 180°C (350°F), mark 4

1. Place the cooked macaroni in a large bowl.
2. Drain the tuna and flake well; add to the macaroni, with the white sauce, cheese and seasonings.
3. Mix together well and place in a greased casserole.
4. Slightly crush the crisps and spread evenly over the top.
5. Bake for 20 mins., and serve at once.

A

B

C

D

E

Blended Sauces

This type of sauce is made by adding a little cold liquid to the thickening agent, usually flour, cornflour or arrowroot, and then adding the hot liquid.

CUSTARD

3 level tbsps custard powder
500ml milk (1pt)
25g sugar (1oz)

1. Put the custard powder into a basin and mix to a thin paste with a little of the cold milk (*photo* A).
2. Heat the remaining milk until boiling and pour on to the blended mixture, stirring constantly to prevent lumps forming (*photo* B).
3. Return the mixture to the pan and bring to the boil, stirring (*photo* C).
4. Cook for 1–2 mins., until the sauce thickens; add the sugar (*photo* D). Serve with fruit pie, etc. (*photo* E).

For a thick custard, increase the custard powder to 4 level tbsps.

JAM SAUCE

4 tbsps raspberry jam
125ml water (¼pt)
2 level tsps cornflour

1. Heat together the jam and water.
2. Blend the cornflour with a little cold water.
3. Pour the heated jam through a sieve on to the cornflour and stir well.
4. Return the sauce to the heat and boil to thicken, stirring.

Serve with steamed or baked puddings.

BUTTERSCOTCH NUT SAUCE

1 tbsp golden syrup
1 level tbsp brown sugar
13g butter (½oz)
2 level tbsps custard powder
125ml water (¼pt)
Lemon juice
2 tbsps chopped nuts

1. Heat together the syrup, sugar and butter in a pan and remove from the heat.
2. Blend the custard powder with the water and add to the pan.
3. Return the mixture to the heat and bring to the boil, stirring.
4. Add a few drops of lemon juice, with the nuts.

Serve hot or cold, with steamed or baked puddings.

FRUIT SAUCE

2 level tsps arrowroot
250ml fruit juice (½pt) from canned fruit

1. Blend the arrowroot with a little of the fruit juice.
2. Heat the remaining fruit juice and pour on to the mixture, stirring.
3. Return the pan to the heat and bring to the boil.

Serve hot, with fruit fritters or fruit puddings.

A

B

C

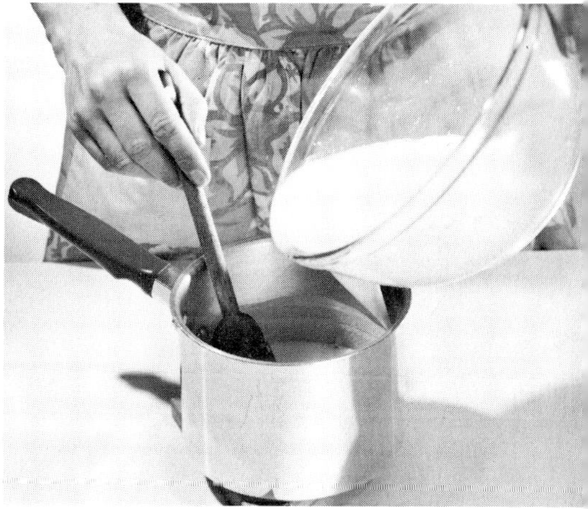

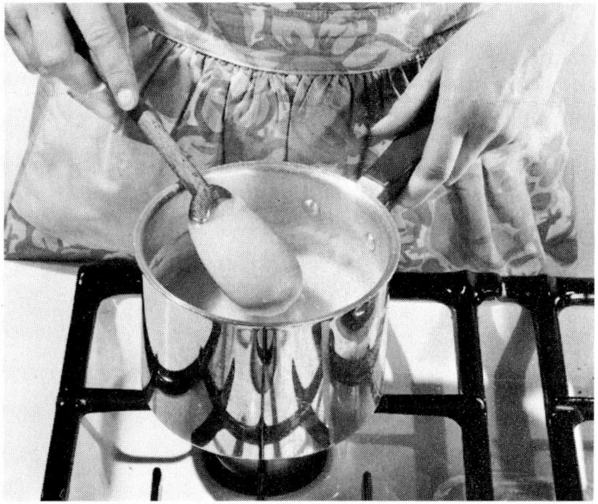

D

E

Hot Milk Puddings

Somewhat different methods are used, according to the size of the cereal grain.

BAKED RICE PUDDING

A small knob of butter
40g rice (1½oz)
25g sugar (1oz)
500ml milk (1pt)
Nutmeg

Oven temperature 150°C (300°F), mark 2

1. Grease a pie dish (2-pt) and put in the washed rice (*photo* A).
2. Add the sugar and milk and stir well (*photo* B).
3. Sprinkle a little grated nutmeg over the pudding.
4. Bake for 2–2½ hrs, until the grain is soft, the milk creamy and the skin golden-brown (*see large photo*).

SEMOLINA PUDDING

500ml milk (1pt)
40g semolina (1½oz)
40g sugar (1½oz)

1. Pour the milk into a saucepan and bring to simmering point.
2. Sprinkle the semolina and sugar over the surface of the milk (*photo* D) and stir continuously with a wooden spoon until the milk boils.
3. Reduce the heat and cook gently for 15–20 mins., stirring occasionally.
4. Pour into a serving dish (*photo* E). If liked, sprinkle with nutmeg (*photo* F). The pudding can then be browned in the oven at 180°C (350°F), mark 4 (*see large photo*).

Sago, Ground Rice and Flaked Rice
Cook like semolina.

VARIATIONS

(*a*) Add 25g cocoa (1oz) to the milk to make a chocolate-flavoured pudding.

(*b*) Dried fruit, e.g., sultanas or currants, and chopped nuts, can be stirred into a pudding as it thickens.

(*c*) Fruit purées or jam can be served with the hot pudding.

(*d*) An Orange Rice Meringue can be made by flavouring the pudding with a can of frozen orange juice and topping with meringue made from 2 egg whites and 75g sugar (3oz)—see p. 58.

(e) Make a Fruit Condé with cold rice pudding, canned peach halves and raspberry jam; divide the pudding between 4 individual glass dishes, place a peach-half in each and pour over warmed, sieved raspberry jam.

A

B

C

D

E

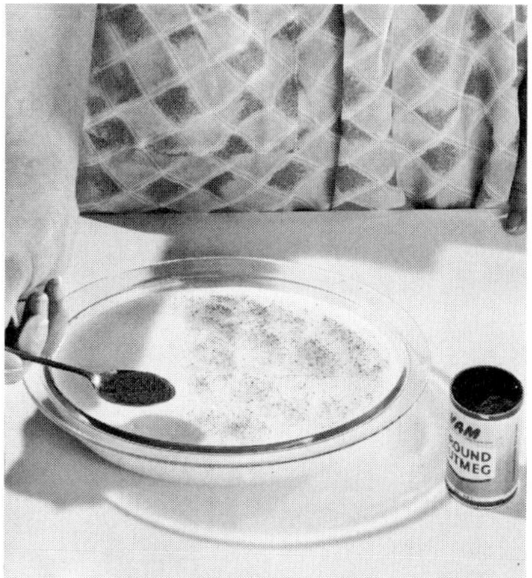

F

G

Cold Milk Puddings

Many packet mixes for cold desserts are available in the shops. They are usually mixed with milk, and are quick and easy to make. Some need no heating, and can be eaten soon after mixing.

LAYERED BLANCMANGE

A pkt of vanilla blancmange powder
3 level tbsps sugar
500ml milk (1pt)
2-3 level tbsps cocoa powder

1. Mix the blancmange powder with the sugar in a basin, add 2 tbsps milk and blend until smooth (*photo* A).
2. Boil the remaining milk in a pan and pour on to the blended mixture, stirring all the time (*photo* B).
3. Return the mixture to the pan and bring gently to the boil, stirring until thick, smooth and shiny (*photo* C).
4. Add the cocoa powder to half the mixture, layer the two flavours into 4 individual glasses and leave to set (*photos* D *and* E).

VARIATIONS

(*a*) Add chopped nuts to a chocolate or coffee blancmange (*photo* E).

(*b*) Layer strawberry blancmange and strawberry jam in individual dishes (*photo* E).

(*c*) Layer blancmange with chopped fruit and jelly to make a sundae; top with whipped cream.

INSTANT 'BLANCMANGE'

A quicker sweet is made by using one of the manufactured instant desserts. Just add 250ml (½pt) or 500ml (1pt) milk, according to the packet directions, and whisk. Divide between the serving dishes and decorate.

BANANA BUTTERSCOTCH PUDDING

1 pkt of butterscotch instant pudding
500ml milk (1pt)
4 bananas, peeled and sliced
2 chocolate digestive biscuits, crushed in a polythene bag
Chocolate vermicelli

Make up the desserts according to the packet instructions. Stir in the bananas and biscuit crumbs. Divide between individual glasses, and decorate with chocolate vermicelli.

VARIATIONS

(*a*) Serve a fruit-flavoured dessert with the appropriate fresh fruit.

(*b*) Serve coffee pudding layered with Chocolate Flake.

(*c*) Use the mixture to fill a flan case and decorate with fruit or whipped cream.

(*d*) Serve with ice cream and chopped nuts.

A

B

C

D

E

Batters I

Batters are made either thin or thick by varying the amount of liquid, according to the dish which you intend to make.

Pouring Batter

100g plain flour (4oz)
½ level tsp salt
1 egg
250ml milk and water (½pt)

Use for Yorkshire pudding, Toad in the hole, Popovers, Fruit batter puddings and Pancakes (see p. 40).

Coating Batter

100g plain flour (4oz)
½ level tsp salt
1 egg
125ml milk and water (¼pt)

Use for coating fish, or fruit for fruit fritters, or for drop scones.

MIXING

1. Sift the flour and salt into a mixing bowl (*photo* A) and make a well in the centre.
2. Drop in the egg and 2 tbsps of the liquid. As you stir, draw the flour from the edges into the egg and liquid. Beat well until smooth (*photos* B *and* C).
3. Gradually add the remaining liquid, beating gently, until the batter is smooth and bubbly (*photo* D).

YORKSHIRE PUDDING OR POPOVERS

25g fat (1oz)
250ml basic pouring batter (½pt)

Oven temperature 220°C (425°F), mark 7

1. Heat the fat in the oven, in a Yorkshire pudding tin or divided between 8 patty tins.
2. Pour in the prepared batter (*photo* E).
3. Bake at the top of the oven for about 40 mins. for a large pudding or 20 mins. for popovers.
4. Turn out (*photo* F), cut into squares if necessary, and serve with roast beef and gravy.

TOAD IN THE HOLE

200g skinless sausages (8oz)
250ml basic pouring batter (½pt)

Oven temperature 220°C (425°F), mark 7

1. Put the sausages in a fairly large shallow tin.
2. Heat in the oven for 10 mins., until some fat has run out of the sausages and become hot.
3. Pour in the batter and bake as above 40–45 mins. Serve at once.

FISH IN BATTER

Oil in a deep-fat pan (see p. 10)
4 pieces of cod
Seasoned flour
125ml basic coating batter (¼pt)
Lemon wedges

1. Heat the oil slowly.
2. Wipe the fish and coat it in seasoned flour.
3. Dip the fish into the batter and, using a skewer, gently lower it into the fat.
4. Fry until golden-brown, then drain well on absorbent kitchen paper.
5. Serve very hot, with lemon wedges and chips (*photo* G).

A

B

C

D

E

F

G

Batters II

PANCAKES

250ml basic pouring batter (½pt)
Cooking fat or oil
Sugar
Lemon wedges

1. Put the batter in a jug.
2. Melt just enough fat in a thick frying pan to coat the bottom and sides. When it is hot, pour off the excess into a basin (*photo* A).
3. Pour in a little batter, tipping the pan so that it thinly covers the bottom (*photo* B).
4. Fry over a moderate heat until golden underneath, shaking the pan gently to prevent sticking.
5. Turn the pancake over carefully with a palette knife (*photos* C *and* D). (Or toss it if you are brave enough.)
6. Cook until the second side is golden. Turn out on to sugared paper, and keep warm in a serving dish.
7. When the pancakes are all cooked, roll them up singly and serve with wedges of lemon (*photo* E).

VARIATIONS—SAVOURY

(*a*) Serve the pancakes filled with a ham and mushroom sauce.
(*b*) Stuff the pancakes with a sauce mixed with sautéed onions, mushrooms and cooked chicken.
(*c*) Fill with a mixture of flaked tuna and canned creamed sweet corn.
(*d*) Stack the pancakes with layers of cooked spinach. Cover the whole with a well flavoured cheese sauce.
(*e*) Fill with mixed cooked vegetables (*photo* F).
(*f*) Stuff with a meat sauce made as follows.

Meat Sauce for Pancakes

25g lard (1oz)
1 onion, peeled and chopped
200g minced meat (8oz)
A 198-g can of tomatoes (7-oz)

1. Melt the fat in a frying pan.
2. Fry the onion gently without browning until soft.
3. Add the meat and cook for 10 mins.
4. Add the tomatoes, season well and cook for a further 10 mins.
5. Serve the stuffed pancakes garnished with watercress and fresh tomatoes.

VARIATIONS—SWEET

(*a*) Replace 25g flour (1oz) in the batter mix by the same amount of cocoa, add 25g sugar (1oz) and prepare as above. Serve filled with whipped cream.
(*b*) Place all the pancakes on a serving dish and serve with an apricot sauce made from 4 level tbsps apricot jam, heated and sieved. Top with 25g chopped nuts (1oz).
(*c*) Layer the pancakes with a can of fruit pie filling. Top with icing sugar and serve with cream.
(*d*) Fill with pineapple chunks and serve with warmed strawberry jam poured over.
(*e*) Fill with fresh strawberries and whipped cream.
(*f*) Make Surprise Pancakes: fill each pancake with a piece of ice cream, roll up and serve with fruit sauce.

A

B

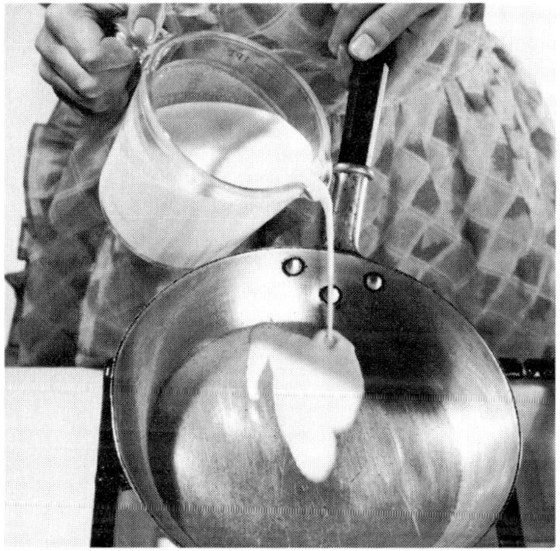

C

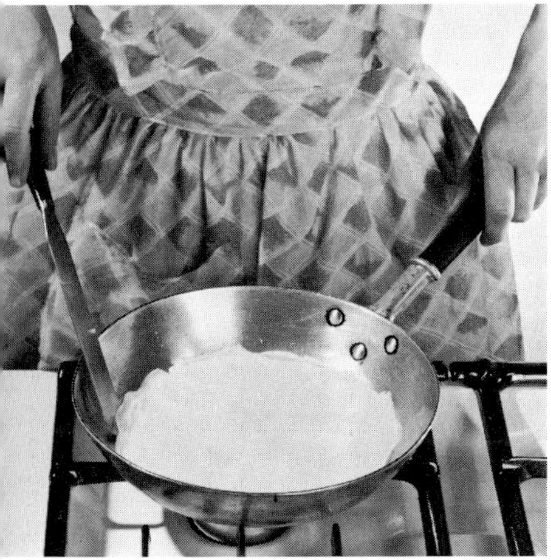

D

E

F

Fruit Salad

Any combination of fresh or canned fruit may be used in this sweet. The salad is nicer if made early in the day, so that the flavours of the fruits blend together.

BASIC FRUIT SALAD RECIPE

1 lemon
2 red-skinned apples
1 banana
2 oranges
50g black grapes (2oz)
100g sugar (4oz)
250ml cold water (½pt)

1. Wash the fruit.
2. Dissolve the sugar in the water in a pan, stir and bring to the boil; when cool, pour into a glass dish.
3. Cut the lemon in half, squeeze out the juice and add it to the sugar syrup.
4. Prepare the apples by cutting into quarters, coring and slicing (*photo* A). Place in the syrup to prevent browning.
5. Peel and slice the banana and add to the syrup (*photo* B).
6. Cut the peel and pith from the oranges, using a sharp knife; cut round the orange in a ½-in. strip, working in a spiral round the fruit and cutting through to the flesh. Hold the orange over a glass dish to catch the juice, and cut it carefully into segments, leaving the membrane and inner pith. Alternatively, the orange may be sliced across the segments (*photo* C). Remove all pips, and place the cut pieces in the syrup.
7. Halve the grapes, remove the pips, using the tip of a knife, and add (*photos* D *and* E).
8. Serve with single cream or whipped double cream.

VARIATIONS

(*a*) When fresh fruit is scarce, or expensive, a can of fruit may be included, e.g., pineapple chunks, peaches, apricots, red or black cherries. In this case, the juice from the can may be used instead of a sugar-and-water syrup.

(*b*) Add some blanched, sliced almonds to the salad to give extra flavour and texture.

(*c*) For a special occasion, add fresh strawberries, and put a dash of liqueur or brandy in the syrup.

(*d*) For a breakfast fruit salad, you can use a mixture of about 400g (1lb) dried fruit such as prunes, apricots and figs; soak them together overnight. Stew them in the same water with 100g sugar (4oz) for 20 mins. until soft. Serve cold.

A

B

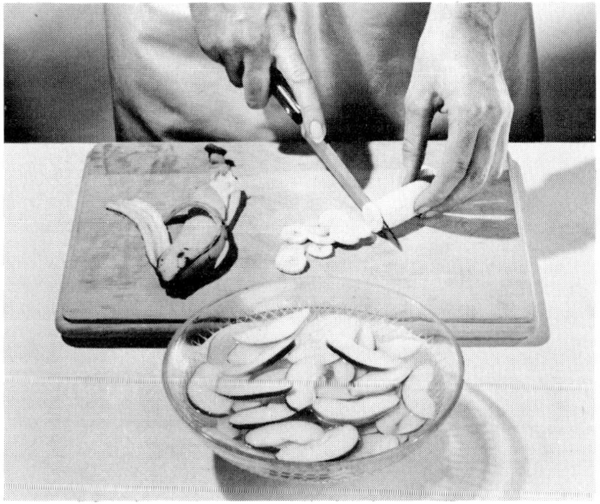

C

D

E

Fruit—Stewed and Puréed

Most fruit can be stewed, and can then be used in various ways.

Basic Recipe for Stewed Fruit

400g cooking apples (1lb), or pears, rhubarb, plums or gooseberries
75g sugar (3oz)
125ml water (¼ pt)

1. Wash, peel and core the fruit and cut into small pieces (*photos* A *and* B) or prepare as required.
2. Dissolve the sugar in the water, add the fruit to the syrup and simmer gently until tender (*photo* B).
3. Unless the fruit is to be puréed, cook it until soft but still whole. Pour into a serving dish and allow to cool. Serve with custard, cream or blancmange.

To Purée Fruit

Cook the fruit—*photo* C—or use canned fruit, drained. Pour into a nylon sieve over a basin (*photo* D), then rub the fruit through, using a wooden spoon. If preferred, use a liquidiser. Stir well, and add a knob of butter, if desired.

Use to make cold desserts.

FRUIT FOOL

A 439-g can of apricots (15-oz), puréed, or other fruit prepared as in basic purée recipe
125ml custard (¼ pt)
125ml double cream (¼ pt)
Chopped nuts

1. Mix the puréed fruit with the custard.
2. Lightly whip the cream and fold it into the mixture.
3. Pile the fool into individual dishes and decorate with nuts.

Note: For a more economical version use all custard. For a gorgeous, extravagant dessert for a party, use all cream; serve with finger biscuits.

APPLE CORNFLAKE CRUNCH

Apple purée (as basic recipe)
40g butter (1½ oz)
2 tbsps golden syrup
25g cornflakes (1oz)
4 tbsps single cream

1. Divide the purée between 4 glass dishes.
2. Heat the butter and syrup in a pan until melted, stir in the cornflakes and mix until evenly coated (*photo* E).
3. Pour a layer of cream over the apple in each dish.
4. Pile the cornflake mixture on top (*photos* F *and* G).

Note: A can of pie filling used in the same way is very good.

VARIATIONS

(*a*) Fruit purée can be put into a flan case and covered with meringue.
(*b*) Mousse can be made by dissolving a lemon jelly in 250ml water (½pt); when it is setting, fold in the fruit purée and then 125ml whipped double cream (¼ pt). Divide between individual dishes and allow to set.

A

B

C

D

E

F

G

Trifle

An attractive sweet that lends itself to a number of variations.

Basic Trifle Recipe

6 individual sponge cakes
Raspberry jam
A small can of peach slices
2 bananas, sliced
375ml custard (3/4 pt)
125ml double cream (1/4 pt)
Chocolate vermicelli

1. Split the sponge cakes and spread with a little jam (*photo* A); cut into pieces and place in a glass bowl.
2. Pour a little of the peach juice over the cakes to moisten.
3. Cover with the peaches and sliced banana (*photo* B).
4. Pour the custard over the fruit and allow to set (*photo* C).
5. Gently whip the cream until it thickens slightly. Spread over the custard and decorate with chocolate vermicelli (*photos* D *and* E).

VARIATIONS

(*a*) For a special occasion, use 1 glass of sherry to moisten the sponge cakes.

(*b*) For a very quick and easy trifle use a jam Swiss roll and pour the contents of a small can of fruit over; make up a packet of vanilla instant dessert and top the trifle with it. Decorate with cream, glacé cherries and angelica.

(*c*) A chocolate trifle can be made using a chocolate Swiss roll, a can of pears and packet of chocolate blanc-mange or instant dessert. Decorate with whipped cream.

TRADITIONAL VICTORIAN TRIFLE

This doesn't contain any fruit. It is rather extravagant to make, but is delicious for a special occasion such as Christmas. An egg custard is normally used, which needs great care, but if you prefer, you can use the packet kind.

Sponge cakes
Ratafias
1 wineglassful sherry
2 tbsps brandy (optional)
3 egg yolks
1 level tbsp sugar
250ml milk (1/2 pt)
125ml double cream (1/4 pt)
Flaked almonds to decorate

1. Place the sponge cakes and ratafia biscuits in a glass dish and soak with the sherry and the brandy.
2. Whisk egg yolks and sugar lightly.
3. Warm milk and pour on to eggs.
4. Strain mixture into top of a double saucepan or a thick-based pan.
5. Stir over a gentle heat until the sauce thickens (DON'T BOIL).
6. Allow to cool slightly and pour over the sponge cakes.
7. Decorate with whipped cream and flaked almonds.

JELLY TRIFLE

Not too rich, so good for children.

4 small sponge cakes
A 311-g can of fruit salad (11-oz)
1/2 a pkt of jelly
250ml thick custard (1/2 pt)
Small sweets to decorate

1. Arrange the cakes in a glass dish.
2. Drain the syrup from the fruit and use (with water if necessary) to make up the jelly.
3. Put the fruit in a layer over the cake and pour the jelly over. Allow to set.
4. Pour the prepared custard over and decorate with small coloured sweets.

A

B

C

D

E

Serving Ice Cream

Ice cream is an ever-popular dessert, and now that it is available in large, resealable cartons, and even in gallon cans for the freezer, it makes the ideal standby for any meal. Though delicious by itself, it is much more exciting with other ingredients. Here are some ideas to try:

With a Sauce

Use a fruit sauce, one of the ready-made bought sauces or a chocolate sauce. (See p. 32 for other sauces.)

Chocolate Sauce (to serve hot or cold)

Melt 50g plain chocolate (2oz) in a basin over hot water, add 13g butter (½oz) and then stir in 1 tbsp milk and 1 tsp vanilla essence. Serve hot, poured over the ice cream.

With Fruit

Ice cream can be served plain with fresh fruit or with canned or frozen fruit. However there are traditional ice cream dishes using fruit plus a sauce and nuts.

BANANA SPLIT

4 bananas
Vanilla ice cream
Chocolate sauce
25g chopped nuts (1oz)

Slice the bananas lengthwise and place on a serving dish with a helping of ice cream in the centre (*photo* A); cover with hot sauce and sprinkle with nuts (*photo* C).

PEARS BELLE HÉLÈNE

A can of pears, drained
Ice cream
125ml whipped cream (¼ pt)
Chopped nuts

Put the pears into 4 individual dishes (*photo* B). Spoon ice cream on and pour the chocolate sauce over. Decorate with whipped cream and chopped nuts (*photo* C).

PEACH MELBA

4 tbsps raspberry jam, sieved
Vanilla ice cream
A small can of peach halves, drained
Chopped walnuts

Warm the jam. Spoon a helping of ice cream into 4 glass dishes, then add 2 peach halves to each. Pour the jam over and sprinkle with walnuts.

OTHER VARIATIONS

(*a*) Use with meringues (see p. 58) and pour a sauce over.
(*b*) Use in pancakes (see p. 40).
(*c*) Make a Baked Alaska (see p. 58).
(*d*) Serve ice cream with chopped jelly.
(*e*) Mix vanilla ice cream with a broken chocolate flake bar.
(*f*) Make Knickerbocker Glory: jelly, fruit, ice cream, sauce and nuts all layered in a tall glass.
(*g*) Serve with home-made fruit salad.
(*h*) Use an 'Arctic Roll'—cut into slices, and decorate with mandarin oranges and whipped cream (*photos* D, E *and* F).
(*i*) You can make your own fruit ice cream by mixing softened ice cream with an equal proportion of softened fruit, e.g., blackberries, raspberries. Fill an ice tray and refreeze for 2 hrs. before serving.

A

B

C

D

E

F

Rubbing-in Method for Cakes and Puddings

The method of mixing fat and flour together, using the fingertips. It is only suitable for recipes using half (or less than half) fat to flour. It is also the method used to make shortcrust pastry. Three typical ways of using it are given below.

Basic Recipe

200g self-raising flour (8oz)
A pinch of salt
100g sugar (4oz)
100g butter (4oz)

1. Sift the flour and salt into a mixing bowl; add the sugar.
2. Add the fat to the flour, cutting it up into small pieces.
3. Using the fingertips, rub in the fat until there are no lumps left and the mixture resembles fine breadcrumbs —over-rubbing produces a greasy result (*photo* A).

FRUIT BUNS (ROCK CAKES)

100g dried fruit (4oz)
25g chopped candied peel (1oz)
1 egg, beaten
2 tbsps milk

Oven temperature 190°C (375°F), mark 5

1. Mix all the ingredients together with a little milk to give a stiff dough (*photos* B *and* C).
2. Spoon the mixture in small piles on to a greased baking sheet (*photo* D).
3. Bake towards the top of the oven for 15–20 mins., until lightly browned (*photo* E).

Variations: Replace the dried fruit by 100g (4oz) chopped dates, chopped glacé cherries, or polka dots.

BANANA NUT BREAD

50g margarine (2oz)
200g self-raising flour (8oz)
A pinch of salt
50g caster sugar (2oz)
50g walnuts, chopped (2oz)
1 egg, beaten
75g golden syrup (3oz)
2 medium-sized bananas, mashed

Oven temperature 180°C (350°F), mark 4

1. Grease an oblong tin 22cm × 10cm (7 ½ in. × 3 ½ in.).
2. Rub the fat into the flour and salt.
3. Stir in the sugar and nuts.
4. Mix together the egg, syrup and bananas, add to the rubbed-in mixture and stir well.
5. Put into the tin, level with a knife and bake for 1 hr.
6. Cool on a wire rack, and serve sliced, with butter and honey.

FRUIT CRUMBLE PUDDING

1. Place a can of fruit pie filling in an ovenproof dish, or prepare 400g fresh fruit (1lb).
2. Make half the basic rubbed-in recipe and sprinkle the mixture (i.e., the 'crumble') on top.
3. Sprinkle with 1 level tbsp Demerara sugar and bake at 190°C (375°F), mark 5, for 20 mins.
4. Serve with cream.

A

B

C

D

E

Creaming Method for Cakes and Puddings

This is the method of beating fat and sugar together to incorporate the air that is necessary to raise the mixture.

Basic Recipe for Victoria Sandwich
100g butter or margarine (4oz)
100g caster sugar (4oz)
2 eggs, beaten
100g self-raising flour (4oz)
2 level tbsps jam
Caster sugar to dredge top

Oven temperature 190°C (375°F), mark 5

1. Grease two 21-cm sandwich cake tins (7-in.) and cut a round of greaseproof paper for each base; grease these also (*photo* A).
2. Cream the fat and sugar together, using a wooden spoon or an electric mixer, until the mixture is almost white and fluffy (*photo* B).
3. Add the eggs a little at a time, beating well after each addition (*photo* C).
4. Lightly fold in half the flour, using a metal spoon, then carefully fold in the rest (*photo* D).
5. Place half the mixture in each tin and level it with a knife (*photo* E).
6. Bake both cakes on the same shelf, in the centre of the oven, for about 20 mins., or until well risen, golden, firm to the touch and beginning to shrink away from the sides of the tin.
7. Turn the cakes out onto a clean tea towel and remove the papers. Invert them on to a cooling tray. (The towel prevents tray marking top of cake.)
8. When they are cool, sandwich together with jam and sprinkle the top of the cake with caster sugar (*photos* F *and* G).

VARIATIONS

(*a*) Chocolate—replace 25g flour (1oz) by the same amount of cocoa. Sandwich together with chocolate sandwich spread or butter cream.

(*b*) Coffee—include 2 level tsps instant coffee or 1 tbsp strong black coffee, adding it with the egg. Sandwich together with coffee butter cream.

(*c*) Orange or Lemon—add 2 level tsps grated rind of 1 orange or lemon. Sandwich together with lemon curd.

(*d*) Fruit Cake—add 25g washed and chopped glacé cherries (1oz), 25g sultanas (1oz), 25g chopped candied peel (1oz) and 50g extra flour (2oz). Bake in an oblong tin at 160°C (325°F) mark 3, for about 1–1¼ hrs.

LEMON SPONGE PUDDING

Juice and grated rind of 1 lemon
50g butter (2oz)
100g caster sugar (4oz)
2 eggs (separated)
250ml milk (½pt)
50g self-raising flour (2oz)

Oven temperature 200°C (400°F), mark 6

1. Add the grated lemon rind to the butter and sugar, and cream the mixture well.
2. Add the egg yolks and beat well.
3. Stir in the milk, lemon juice and flour.
4. Whisk the egg whites stiffly, fold into the mixture and pour into a 750-ml ovenproof dish (1½-pt).
5. Stand the dish in a shallow tin of water and cook near the top of the oven for about 45 mins., or until the top is set and firm to the touch.

Note: This pudding separates out during the cooking into a sauce layer with a sponge topping.

A

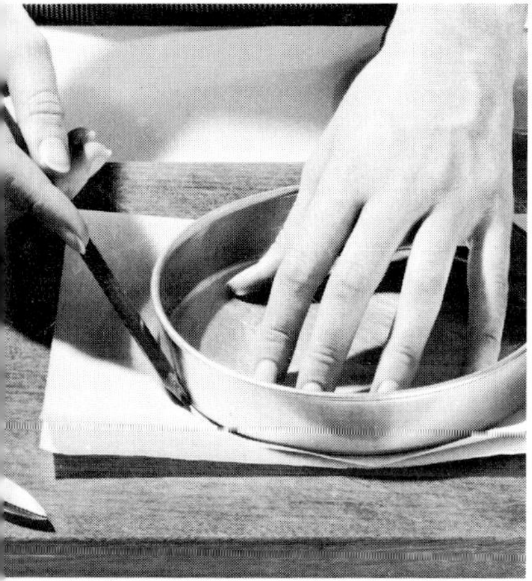

B

C

D

E

F

G

One-step Method for Cakes and Puddings

Basic Recipe—Small Buns

100g self-raising flour (4oz)
1 level tsp baking powder
100g soft margarine (4oz)
100g caster sugar (4oz)
2 eggs
1 tbsp milk

Oven temperature 190°C (375°F), mark 5

MAKES 24 BUNS

1. Have paper baking cases ready.
2. Sift the flour and baking powder into a mixing bowl.
3. Add all the other ingredients and beat well together for 1 min.
4. Divide the mixture between the paper cases and bake on a baking sheet near the top of the oven for 15–20 mins. The buns should be well-risen and firm.
5. Remove from oven and place on a cooling rack.
6. When they are cool, decorate with glacé icing or butter cream (see recipes on p. 56).

VARIATIONS

(a) *Chocolate*—replace 25g flour (1oz) by the same amount of cocoa powder.
(b) *Queen Cakes*—add 25g sultanas (1oz) to the mixture.

Any of the recipes using the creaming method can be made by the one-step method if soft margarine is substituted for butter.

JAM SPONGE PUDDING

2 level tbsps jam (or golden syrup or marmalade)
125g self-raising flour (5oz)
75g margarine (3oz)
75g caster sugar (3oz)
1 egg, beaten
2 tbsps milk to mix

1. Boil some water in a steamer or saucepan.
2. Grease a 750-ml pudding basin (1½-pt) and put in the jam.
3. Mix all the other ingredients together, beat well and put into the basin, making sure it is only two-thirds full (*photo* A).
4. Cover with foil or with greaseproof paper secured with string (*photo* B).
5. Steam for 2 hrs.
6. Turn out on to a serving plate and serve with custard (*photo* C).

VARIATIONS

(a) *Chocolate*—replace 25g flour (1oz) by the same amount of cocoa powder; serve with chocolate sauce.
(b) *Fruit Cap Pudding*—place half a can of fruit pie filling in the basin before adding mixture; serve with cream.
(c) *Castle Puddings*—divide the basic mixture between 4 dariole moulds and bake at 180°C (350°F), mark 4, for 15–20 mins.; serve with jam sauce.
(d) *Upside-down Pudding*—put 4 canned pineapple rings with a glacé cherry in each in the base of a 21-cm cake tin (7-in.). Pour over them 3 tbsps warmed golden syrup. Cover with the basic mixture (*photo* D). Bake at 180°C (350°F), mark 4, for 40–45 mins. Place a serving dish over tin and turn both upside-down (*photos* E *and* F). Serve with the pineapple juice heated and thickened with arrowroot (see p. 32).

A

B

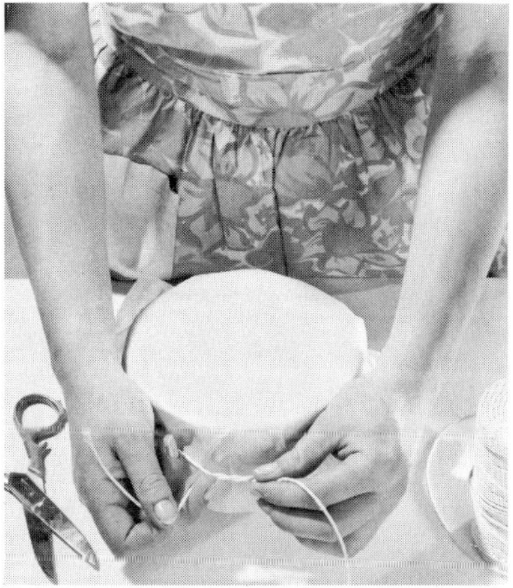

C

D

E

F

Cake Decorating

A plain Victoria sandwich can be decorated in many ways. Before starting, make sure the cake is flat. It may be necessary to turn it upside-down and then use the base. Brush away any crumbs and place on a cooling tray or upturned dinner plate, so that you can turn it round easily. Prepare *all* decorations before starting.

BUTTER CREAM

100g icing sugar (4oz)
50g butter or margarine (2oz)
Flavouring

1. Sift the sugar into a basin.
2. Add the butter, cut in small pieces.
3. Cream together with a wooden spoon until light and creamy.
4. Add a flavouring such as a few drops of vanilla essence; 1 tbsp melted chocolate; 2 level tsps instant coffee dissolved in 1 tsp hot water; or finely grated orange or lemon rind.
5. Add food colouring if you wish; use with care, as these colourings are strong—drip it into a teaspoon first.
6. Use in one of the following ways:
   As a Filling: Spread the butter cream over the lower half of the cake, then put the top half in place.
   As a Topping: The cake can be sandwiched together with jam and the top then covered with butter cream. Spread it evenly over the surface and mark a pattern with a fork or skewer (*photo* A). Other decorations can be added. Alternatively, the cake can be covered with butter cream and then the sides can be rolled in chopped nuts and the top decorated.
   For Piped Decoration: Use a small star nozzle for special cakes.

GLACÉ ICING

200g icing sugar (8oz)
Water to mix
Flavouring and/or colouring as needed

1. Sift the sugar into a basin.
2. Add some warm water, 1 tsp at a time, stirring until all the sugar is mixed in and the icing is thick enough to coat the back of a spoon.
3. Add flavouring and/or colouring, if used, as for Butter Cream.

VARIATIONS

(*a*) The cake sides can be brushed with melted jam and then rolled in chopped nuts or coconut (*photo* C).

(*b*) Coat the cake top with glacé icing, divide into quarters and fill two with chopped nuts; add a border of larger pieces of nut (*photo* D).

(*c*) Fairy Cakes can be decorated with icing and/or butter cream. By using a different design on each cake, an attractive array (*photo* B) can be quickly produced—for example:
White glacé icing and glacé cherries
Chocolate glacé icing and Smarties
Chocolate glacé icing and chocolate vermicelli
Butter cream in 'Chocolate Top-hat Cakes' (*photo* E)

Party Cakes

(*a*) A Chocolate Victoria Sandwich Cake can be made into a Black Forest Gâteau simply by using a can of cherry pie filling. Sandwich the cake together with whipped cream and half the pie filling. Pile the rest of the filling on top, and pipe with whipped cream; decorate with grated chocolate.

(*b*) Top a chocolate sandwich cake with marshmallows and grill lightly (*photo* F).

A

B

C

D

E

F

Meringues and Meringue Sweets

Meringue is stiffly whisked egg white, with sugar folded in, which is dried out in the oven.

Basic Meringue Recipe

2 egg whites
100g caster sugar (4oz)

Oven temperature 120°C (250°F), mark ½

1. Line a baking sheet with silicone paper or greaseproof paper, lightly oiled (*photo* A).
2. Separate the eggs in this way: Break one into a saucer, place a tiny glass or egg cup over the yolk, invert, and pour the white into a basin (*photo* B). Repeat. The egg whites should be completely free from shell and yolk.
3. Whisk the egg whites until they stand up in peaks (*photo* C).
4. Sprinkle half the sugar over the whites and whisk until the mixture is very stiff indeed (*photo* D).
5. Fold in the remaining sugar carefully with a metal spoon or a spatula (*photo* E).
6. Pile in spoonfuls, or pipe on to the paper (*photo* F).
7. Dry in the centre of the oven until crisp, but still white (about 2½ hrs.).
8. To use:
   (*a*) Sandwich together with whipped double cream (*photo* G).
   (*b*) Place flat side down in a glass serving dish and decorate with fruit and cream.
   (*c*) Serve sandwiched in pairs with a slice of ice cream.

MERINGUE-TOPPED PUDDINGS

Many basic puddings can be made more exciting by adding a meringue topping. Semolina pudding can be covered with a layer of jam and then meringue. (The egg yolks are generally used in the pudding itself.) A fruit flan can also be topped with meringue. The meringue used for puddings is made with less sugar, because it does not need to be as stiff or dry as for individual meringues.

Basic Meringue Topping Recipe

2 egg whites
50g caster sugar (2oz)

Oven temperature 150°C (300°F), mark 2

1. Make the meringue as already described.
2. Pile on to the pudding, covering it completely. Fork the meringue into peaks.
3. Bake for ½ hr., till the meringue is a faint gold colour.

Baked Alaska

1 sponge flan or 1 layer of Victoria sandwich cake
1 block of ice cream
Fruit—either canned or fresh (strawberries are lovely)
2 egg whites
100g caster sugar (4oz)

Oven temperature 230°C (450°F), mark 8

1. Place the cake on an ovenproof plate.
2. Place the ice cream in the centre and the fruit on top.
3. Cover the whole with meringue, making sure it touches the plate all round.
4. 'Peak' the meringue with a fork and 'flash-bake' for 2 mins., until coloured. Serve this spectacular dessert immediately.

Note: The meringue is not supposed to be hard after 'flash-baking'.

A

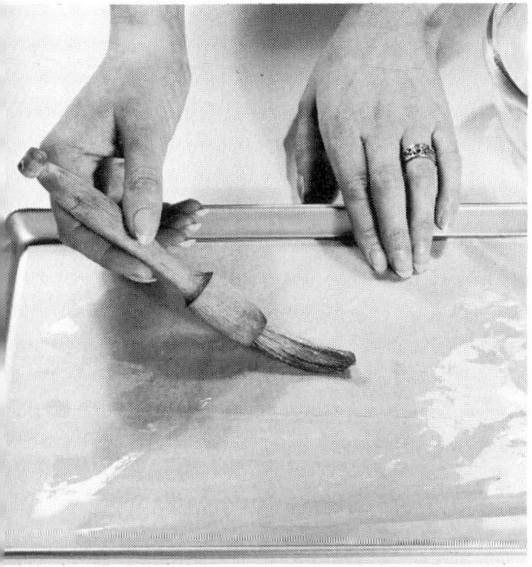

B

C

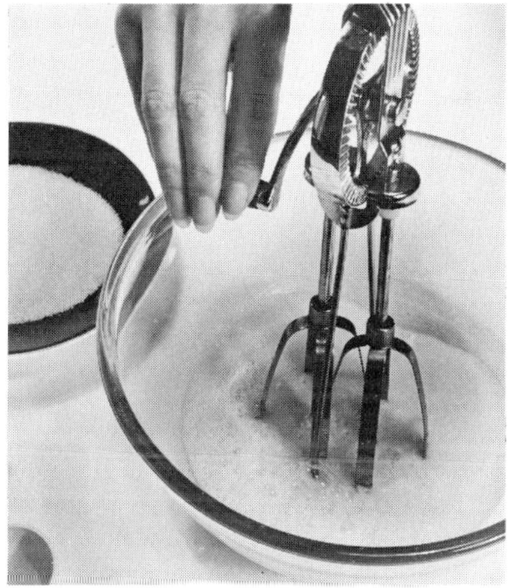

D

E

F

G

Sandwiches

Simple kinds are ideal for snacks and packed lunches, and the more elaborate varieties for parties. Many different fillings and different types of bread can of course be used. Presentation is most important: a cheese sandwich for a packed lunch, for instance, should be quite different from a dainty tea-time sandwich. Open sandwiches are suitable for a buffet, or a special lunch-time meal, because they look very colourful.

Breads and Alternatives

Brown sliced; white sliced; wholemeal; rye; French stick; crisp or soft rolls; crispbreads.

Fillings

The filling depends upon the particular occasion. It is important that sandwiches for a packed lunch should be nutritious. Fillings for tea-time sandwiches are not quite so vital, as this is not usually a main meal. But whatever the occasion, a good balance of texture and flavour is essential. Here are some suggestions: Beef and horseradish; Pork and apple; Salmon and chopped cucumber; Corned beef and pickle; Cheese and chutney; Grated cheese and celery; Ham and mustard; Cream cheese, onion rings and chopped pepper; Tuna fish and mayonnaise; Cooked Steaklets with fried onion rings (*photo* B).

For breakfast, try a sandwich of grilled bacon and scrambled eggs.

There are various manufactured fillings available, e.g., peanut butter, Marmite, pastes and pâtés, chocolate spread, jam and honey.

SANDWICH-MAKING

1. Prepare all the fillings; bind all savoury fillings with salad cream or cream to give a good consistency, season well and add a flavouring where appropriate.
2. Slice the bread if necessary.
3. Soften the butter before spreading it evenly over the slices of bread, using a round-bladed knife. Soft margarines are ideal for sandwiches.
4. Put a generous amount of filling on one slice, then cover with a second slice.
5. Press the covering slices firmly in place and cut the sandwiches into squares or triangles, using a sharp knife. For a formal occasion, cut off all the crusts.

Fancy shapes can be made by using pastry cutters. You can layer several slices, with different fillings, and cut into fingers or triangles (*photo* E).

VARIATIONS

(*a*) Toasted sandwich (ideal for snacks): Make up a sandwich using cheese and ham, bacon and cheese, or cheese and tomato. Press well together and grill on both sides until brown; serve hot—topped if you like with a fried egg (*photos* A *and* C).

(*b*) Any left-over sandwiches are delicious fried in a little butter until golden-brown.

(*c*) Snack Roll: Use a long French roll, slice it along one side and fill with slices of meat, hard-boiled egg and tomato; ideal for picnics.

(*d*) Double-deckers: Aim at a good contrast of fillings (*photo* C).

(*e*) Danish Open Sandwiches: Butter one slice of bread or crispbread, cover with a lettuce leaf and arrange cold meats, cheese, vegetables, mayonnaise or fruit (e.g. apple, banana, pineapple) on top (*photo* D).

A

B

C

D

E

Hot Drinks

TEA

1. Boil some fresh water in the kettle, pour a little into the tea-pot and leave to warm, then throw this water away.
2. Put the tea in the pot, allowing 1 level tsp per person and 1 extra 'for the pot'.
3. Pour on the really boiling water, three-quarters filling the pot; leave for 2 mins. to brew before pouring out.
4. Serve with fresh milk and sugar—granulated or cube—if required. Some people drink tea with a slice of lemon instead of milk; this lemon tea is served in a tall glass, if available, and is very refreshing in summer.

Guests should be asked how they like their tea, and should be allowed to serve themselves with sugar.

COFFEE

You can make coffee in several ways, using various types of equipment. Whichever method you follow, you must have freshly ground coffee, as the flavour is lost if coffee is stored too long. Allow 4 level tbsps coffee to 1pt freshly boiled water. Coffee is usually served with milk—hot, not boiled—generally 1 part milk to 2 parts coffee. Brown or Demerara sugar is usually served.

For special occasions coffee can be served with cream. The sugar (if used) is stirred in, and then the cream is floated on top of the coffee; the hot coffee is drunk through the cool cream.

Making Coffee in a Jug

1. Warm the jug with boiling water and then put in the coffee.
2. Pour on the fast-boiling water and stir well.
3. Cover the jug and infuse for 5 mins., stirring occasionally to settle the grounds.
4. Serve at once (*see large photo*).

Other Methods of Coffee-making

You can also make coffee using a percolator (*photos* C and D), by the vacuum Cona method (*photos* E and F) or by the filter method (*photos* A and B). Follow the instructions given with the particular apparatus.

INSTANT COFFEE

The quickest way. Place 1 level tsp of instant coffee in a cup, fill three-quarters full with boiling water, and top up with hot or cold milk.

HOT CHOCOLATE

This can be made with either drinking chocolate or cocoa. Use all milk, or half milk and half water; heat the liquid without boiling in a saucepan. Whisk in the drinking chocolate or the blended cocoa, and pour into beakers to serve. For special occasions, a topping of whipped cream is delicious.

MOCHA

Can be made by adding 1 level tsp instant coffee and 1 level tsp drinking chocolate to a cup or mug of hot milk.

A

B

C

D

E

F

G

Index